A
Crown
Growing Out
of My
Head

WRITTEN AND ILLUSTRATED BY:

KASIMAH ROYALTY EL-AMIN

Balboa Press books may be ordered through booksellers or by contacting:

Balboa Press
A Division of Hay House
1663 Liberty Drive
Bloomington, IN 47403
www.balboapress.com
844-682-1282

ISBN: 979-8-7652-2876-0 (sc)
ISBN: 979-8-7652-2877-7 (e)

Print information available on the last page.

Balboa Press rev. date: 05/12/2022

This book is dedicated to my Inner Child "Sima", who went through a rough healing process & made it through the fires & storms of life. To my husband Rynell & all of my Ancestors, if it wasn't for your knowledge, love & support, my healing would have never taken place. Also this dedication is to my grandchildren Aaliyah, Angelo, Asad, Kingston & Amari. Always Love Yourself, Love Every Part Of You, Knowing That You Come From An Ancient, Royal Bloodline Of Kings & Queens. Thank You Great Spirit, Great Mother, ASHE!!

Aaliyah loved standing in the big mirror in her bathroom looking at herself, admiring her huge, shiny afro puffs that are a beautiful sandy brown color like her fathers short curly hair & her soft, chocolate, brown skin, kissed by the sun, identical to her mothers complexion. She loved her full lips & nose that came together making a perfect combination of her mother & fathers facial features. Everyone always told her how pretty her brown eyes were & that she had cat eyes but looking at her pet Siamese cat Mackeveli she failed to see any resemblance between her eyes & the cats.

Aaliyah was now 9 years of age & was enjoying her very first slumber party at her house with 2 of her friends Jessica & Zaria, wearing their favorite, cartoon pajamas, eating lots of pizza, chips & tons of sweet, sugary snacks that normally couldn't be eaten before dinner. Her mother Lisa frantically ran around trying to keep the children happy. Constantly cleaning, trying to keep things in order, while doing her best to at the same time be fun & entertaining with her daughter's young guest.

MOM
LISA

ZARIA

JESSICA

While in the bathroom, standing in the mirror, the one question in Aaliyah's mind was why did her hair grow so curly, making it so hard to comb sometimes? Especially when it gets wet. Also, why couldn't her hair be like most of the ladies that she sees on television? She had just finished doing her afro puffs & her arms were super tired being her long, thick, tight curls were a challenge & not willing to cooperate at times.

AALIYAH

Aaliyah's biggest question was, why is her Chinese friend Jessica's hair so stringy, straight & seemed much easier to manage? When all of her friends at the slumber party were getting ready for breakfast that morning she noticed that it took Jessica only 3 minutes to comb her hair & when they were in the swimming pool she noticed how easily Jessica was able to comb right through her hair & put it into a ponytail, all in 1 second flat with no struggles, just like the ladies on television & in all of those shampoo commercials.

Aaliyah knew that she was beautiful, people told her that all of the time but today she decided that she wanted hair like Jessicas. Straight hair that blew in the wind & gave a comb & brush absolutely no trouble. She had never thought about it before until today watching her friend Jessica's hair bouncing & blowing, giving her friend no problems from the moment that she woke up until the moment she went to sleep. Aaliyah thought her friend Jessica was so lucky to have such straight hair. Aaliyah decided to talk to her mother about it after dinner that night, right before they would all sit to enjoy a movie.

Finishing a game of Candyland with her friends & then winning a game of Pin The Tail On The Donkey, dinner was finally served as Aaliyah & her friends sat at the dining table, chatting about the many things they would do at school on Monday. Talking about the boys that they thought were rude & how their recesses & playtimes at school just wasn't long enough. Finally dinner was done & Aaliyah's friends all went to wash their hands & began piling into the living room to prepare for the movies. While Aaliyah's mother was finishing up the dinner dishes after the delicious meal of spaghetti & meatballs, Aaliyah thought that this would be the perfect time to talk to her mother about her problems with having thick, curly hair & how they should immediately devise a plan to make her hair look more like Jessica's hair.

Walking into the kitchen, Aaliyah dug into the pocket of her pink, Barbie bathrobe, grabbing the miniature Reese Peanut Butter cup she had gotten out of the candy bowl earlier. Quickly with practiced skill, she peeled off the wrapper & popped it into her mouth, savoring the moment as the chocolate melted on her tongue, mixing with the peanut butter. As she climbed onto the tall stool that was sitting beside the counter where her mother was standing she asked while licking the peanut butter & chocolate from the roof of her mouth, "mom why is my hair so different from Jessica's hair?

Lisa put down the plate she was washing, looking down at her daughter's beautiful, smooth face & asked, "what do you mean honey"? "Well", Aaliyah said looking up into her mothers eyes, "I want my hair to be straight, I want it to blow in the wind when I run like the girls on television, I want to be able to go swimming & not have a thick, curly afro afterwards.

"Look mom, Aaliyah said, jumping off of the stool with excitement, "did you know it only took 2 seconds for Jessica to comb her hair this morning"? I mean Jessica seriously brushed her hair in 5 seconds & was completely finished before everyone else". "If I could do that with my hair, Aaliyah said, "I could get a lot of extra sleep in the morning, especially on school days & it wouldn't hurt so much when you comb it sometimes. Especially after you wash it". "Really mom, I hate getting my hair washed," Aaliyah said, poking out her full bottom lip & crossing her arms over her chest pouting. Then leaning her head to the side thinking, Aaliyah asked, "is that why you wear wigs & fake hair sometimes mom because you want hair like Jessica too?

Her mother tried hard not to laugh but failed. She laughed so hard that Aaliyah started smiling as she began wondering to herself what was so darn funny? Lisa finally stopped laughing & while stroking Aaliyah's cheek, she smiled & told Aaliyah that the reason she wore wigs & fake hair sometimes is because she likes to try different styles that she could never do with her natural hair without damaging her beautiful curls with heat, chemicals or other things. Aaliyah's mother explained that she actually loves her beautiful, all natural hair & that she wouldn't trade it for the world.

Aaliyah, looking confused, asked her mother, "then why if you love your hair so much, why don't you ever wear it in an afro or afro puffs to work or outside in public like me"? Lisa thought about that for a minute & said "well honey, honestly, sometimes my days are so busy that it is just easier for me to put on a wig or some fake hair, that way I can have more time to do special things with you, Lisa said softly kissing Aaliyah on the nose.

Holding Aaliyah's face in her warm hands, she said, "baby, never think that I don't like my natural hair just because I wear wigs or try different styles with fake hair because I truly do love my hair very much". You too must love your hair Aaliyah because it is your African Crown. Taking Aaliyah by the shoulders, she turned her daughter completely towards her so that Aaliyah was looking at her mother, eye to eye, saying in a firm voice, "your hair is amazing Aaliyah. Your African crown is like a beautiful plant, so it grows straight up in the air, reaching for the sun just like the flowers, the grass & the trees. Your tight curls hold galactic, ancient information. Your hair is an antenna to communicate with the stars, so it grows upwards instead of growing down & straight like Jessica's hair.

Your hair is alive Aaliyah & that is why we have to feed your hair things like olive oil, coconut oil, carrot oil, shea butter, eggs, mayonnaise, honey for conditioner & other foods to keep it well fed & healthy. Your hair loves to eat because it is Alive. Aaliyah, your hair is a precious gift from The Great Spirit. It is a beautiful jewel, reaching to the cosmos, growing curly out of your scalp so that you can receive divine messages & hear the Great Spirit's voice much clearer. In Africa our hair grew thick & curly to protect our scalps from the hot sun too but it also represents a Magical Crown. Your Crown represents the truth of African people, being the first people ever created on this planet earth.

Lisa sat down on a stool beside Aaliyah asking her, "did you notice that every other race of people that is on planet earth has straight, stringy hair like Jessicas? Aaliyah had never thought about this before but now that she thought about it, she realized it was true. Her friend Tracy who was Mexican had straight, stringy hair & her friend Amy who is Chinese also had this type of hair. Well no, Aaliyah said, I never really paid attention; "is that because we are different than everyone else '' Aaliyah asked pondering this thought?

"Yes, her mother said, ``very different & very special. We are the first people ever created so we naturally have Crowns growing out of our heads. Aaliyah's mother explained how the African people were the first people ever to walk this planet & that the bible stories & everyone who is spoken of in the Quran & Bible stories are all African people. You are made from stars, Lisa said, stardust, protons, neutrons, electrons & many other powerful elements from our great galaxy. We are carbon, "Etheric'' beings that naturally communicate with the galaxy through our hair & our melanin. This is why our skin is dark like the galaxy. We have tons of magic inside of us Aaliyah, Lisa said smiling, we have Black Girl Magic".

Laughing, Aaliyah jumped up, spinning in a circle on the balls of her feet yelling, "Yes, Black Girl Magic"!! "You got that right, '' Lisa said laughing at her daughter's antics. The African woman gave birth to everyone that you see on this planet today, Lisa said, & I do mean Everyone. Every race & skin color that you see comes from the African woman". "The African woman is the first King & Queen also The Mother of Everything & Everybody. This is why she wears "A Crown That Grows Out Of Her Head" & scalp, so that everyone who sees her Crown knows that she is the Queen Of Everything.

Aaliyah loved this explanation regarding her hair & began stroking her soft afro puffs as if for the first time, appreciating her powerful curls. Suddenly, concerned about her friends, she asked her mother, "but what about Jessica, why doesn't she have a crown growing out of her head too? Honestly mom, Aaliyah said, I really think all of my friends should have a magical crown like mine? "Well", Lisa said laughing, "there can only be one King & Queen at a time & you my love are The Chosen One. You are also a part of a historical, ancient, Royal bloodline", which also makes you Royalty.

"Wow", Aaliyah said while taking another peanut butter cup out of her pocket & popping it into her mouth, "so I can really communicate with the stars, the galaxy & my hair is alive like a plant, Aaliyah asked intrigued with this new information? "Yes", her mother said, "so you must love your beautiful, curly hair & all of its magic because your hair is the first hair ever created, hair of Kings & Queens. Your hair comes from your royal, African bloodline, your Ancestors, your hair represents ancient, magical powers. Aaliyah, your hair is your Crown, do you understand that, Lisa asked? Yes, Aaliyah said, I do understand now & I love my magical hair. Even though it is harder to comb sometimes, Aaliyah said, I love my Crown & I think that I want to keep it now. Well good, her mother said giggling softly to herself, "I'm glad to hear that.

Finally all of the dishes were washed & Aaliyah could hear her friends in the living room laughing at something on the television & playing games. "Okay", Lisa said, "Let's get this popcorn into these bowls so that we can all watch the new movie Cinderella 2 because it is getting kind of late". Soon after all of the popcorn was full of butter & in the bowls, Aaliyah & her mother were both heading into the living room when Aaliyah stopped & said, "Mom I love my hair & I would Never want it to be like anyone else's hair ever again. "Good", Lisa said as they both began passing out the popcorn to Aaliyah's friends, "Is everyone ready for a movie? Lisa yelled.. "Yeeees", they all screamed as Aaliyah began to put Cinderella 2 into the DVD player.

As Aaliyah was getting everything set up with pillows & more snacks, she saw her mother walking out of the living room & heading upstairs yelling," Get Cozy Lades". Lisa secretly smiled & mumbled to herself, "it's going to be a loong, very special night.". It was only 10 minutes into the movie when Aaliyah saw her mother walking back into the living room with sparkling costume jewelry for everyone. Costume jewelry that she got on sale at a place called Costume City, where she always bought all of Aaliyah's party favorites. With all of the excitement going on, Aaliyah also noticed that her mother had taken off her wig & her hair was now combed out & styled into a perfectly shaped, round, brown afro. Sitting down next to Aaliyah, Lisa whispered in her daughter's ear, "Just thought I would wear my Crown to the movies tonight". Smiling, Aaliyah leaned against her mother, smelling that familiar, comforting lavender & vanilla fragrance coming off of her mothers skin, thinking how lucky she was to be the King & Queen of Everything. To have a Crown that actually grows out of her head. All of the things that her mother told her that evening about her hair were actually much better & more interesting to think about than watching Cinderella 2 right now. Right now, all Aaliyah could think about was the magic in her hair, the stardust underneath her skin, Her Black Girl Magic & "The Crown Growing Out Of Her Head". "The End"... or Shall We Say, "The Beginning" #Ashe #Ayibobo

The Magic In Our Hair Has Historically Made An Appearance, Showing Its True Nature, Shining Above The Rest. Jesus Had Long, Wool Locs, Buddha Had The African Nubian Knots, Tied Into A Bun On Top Of His Head etc. For Just A Minute, Forget About Style, Fashion & Trend, Imagine How Beautiful & Strong Your Hair Would Be Right Now If You Had Never Gotten A Perm Or A Process, Damaging Your Antennas. Each Strand Of Your Hair Connects You To The Spirit / God Realms, The Stars & The Galaxy. Our Hair Is One Of Our Highest Forms Of Technology & Magic. Just As The Coils & Wire In Your Computer & Phone Hold Information, Well So Does Your Hair. Actually, The Curler Your Hair Is, The Better It Holds Information From The Divine Realms Of The Universe. So The Curlier Your Hair Is, The Better, Though In This Country A Lot Of People Didn't Know The Science Of African Hair, So We Were Led To Believe That The Longer & The More Straight Your Hair Was, The Better. Our Hair Holds Our Perceptions & Ideas, That Is Why Historically, When Colonizers Would Conquer A Region & Enslave Its Natives, They Would Always Cut Off The Captives / Slaves Hair, Taking Away Their Perceptions & Ideas, Putting Them Under New Ways Of Thinking, Programming The New Hair That Grows On The Slaves Head With Fear, Hate, Trauma Etc. African Women Are Very Powerful, The Original Mothers Of Earth / Of The Motherland & So We Were Forced / Taught To Perm, Straighten & Kill Our Hair Which In Return Kills Its Ability To Receive Or Hold Information. Our Hair Is Sacred & You May See A Lot Of People Covering Their Hair To Protect Their Energy & To Block Out Unclean, Worldly Or Negative Information That Can Attach Itself To Your Hair / Antennas, Causing Confusion, Anxiety, Depression & Basically "Static" In Your Connection To The Galaxy, The Great Mother / Spirit. So From Today, Moving Forward, Honor Your African Crown, Embrace Your Bloodline, Know ThySelf, Teaching Your Children By Example To Love The Crown Growing Out Of Their Head. Ashe, Ashe, Ashe!!

A SALUTE TO HISTORIC
AFRICAN KINGS & QUEENS

Printed in the United States
by Baker & Taylor Publisher Services